COLOR QUEST

W9-AZT-390

Extreme Coloring Challenges to Complete

JOANNA WEBSTER

Reveal the 30 stunning pictures in this book by following the color codes.

The pages are perforated so you can pull out and display each intricate image when you have completed it.

Don't worry if you don't have pens or pencils that exactly match the color key on the left-hand edge of each picture. Darker colors can be achieved by applying more pressure with a pencil, and lighter hues by pressing gently. With pens you can create darker shades by layering the ink. You can also create new, unique colors by blending two shades together. You don't even have to use the colors suggested—choose your own palette! On some of the pages you will notice blank shapes without numbers inside. These should be left white.

There is a small, finished version of each image at the back of the book, just in case you can't wait to find out what you are coloring in.

Visit *www.mombooks.com/activities* to see larger solutions for each puzzle.

BARRON'S

First edition for North America published in 2016 by Barron's Educational Series, Inc.

First published in Great Britain in 2015 by Michael O'Mara Books Limited, 9 Lion Yard, Tremadoc Road, London SW4 7NQ

Copyright © Michael O'Mara Books, 2015

Edited by: Jonny Marx
Illustrations by:
　Joanna Webster
Designed by: Jack Clucas
Cover design by:
　Angie Allison and
　John Bigwood

All inquiries should be addressed to:
Barron's Educational Series, Inc.
250 Wireless Boulevard
Hauppauge, New York 11788
www.barronseduc.com

ISBN: 978-1-4380-0856-1

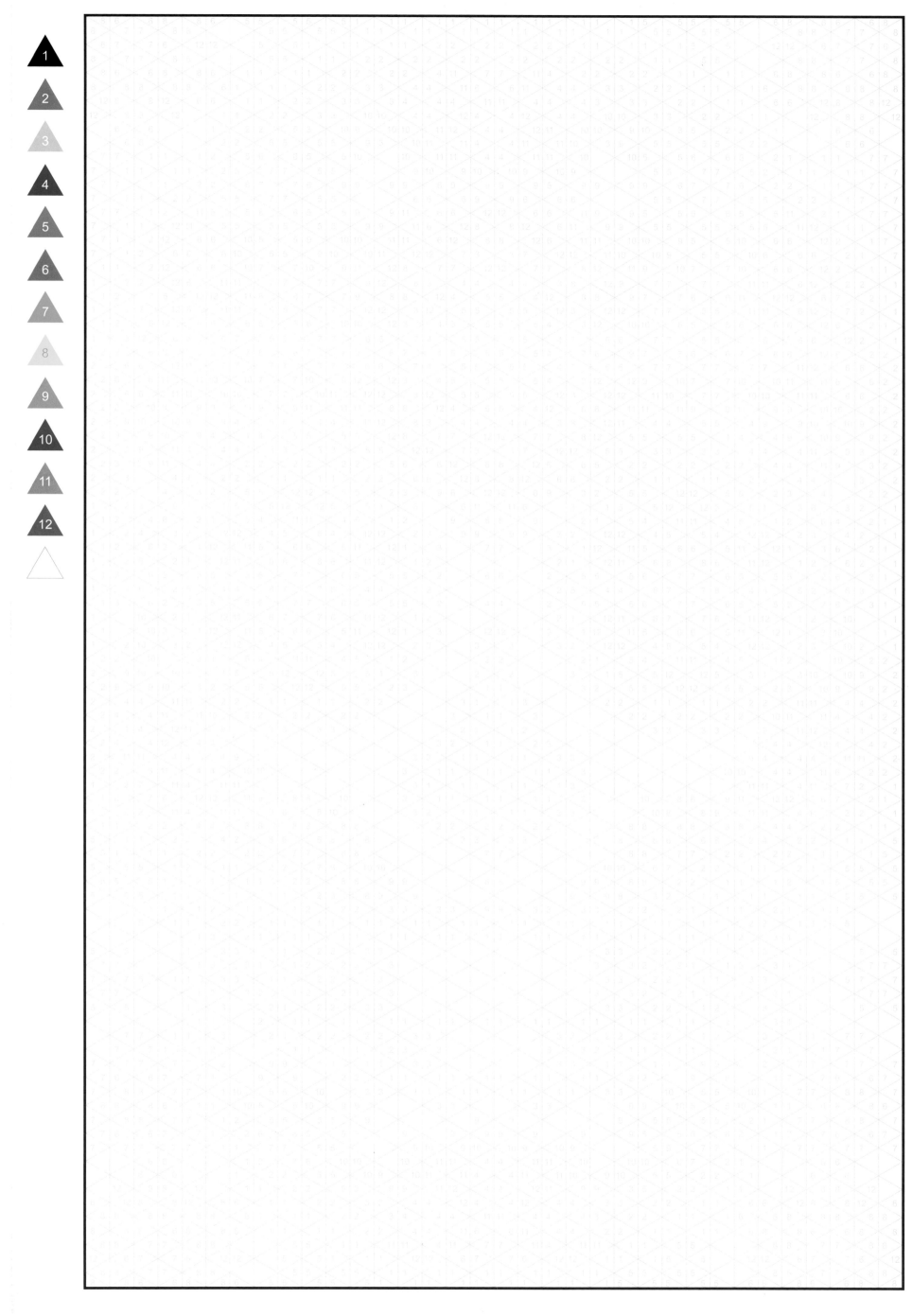

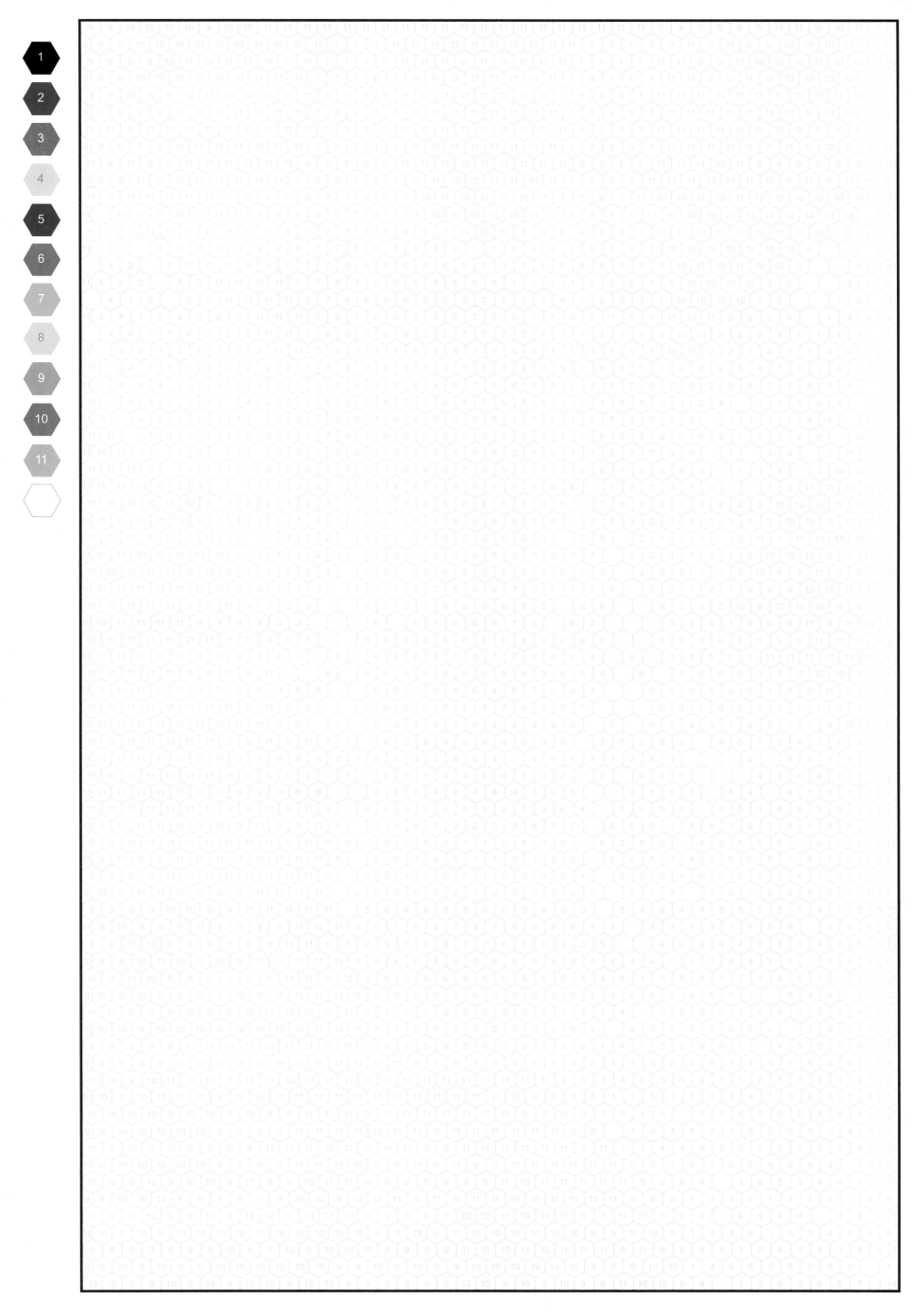

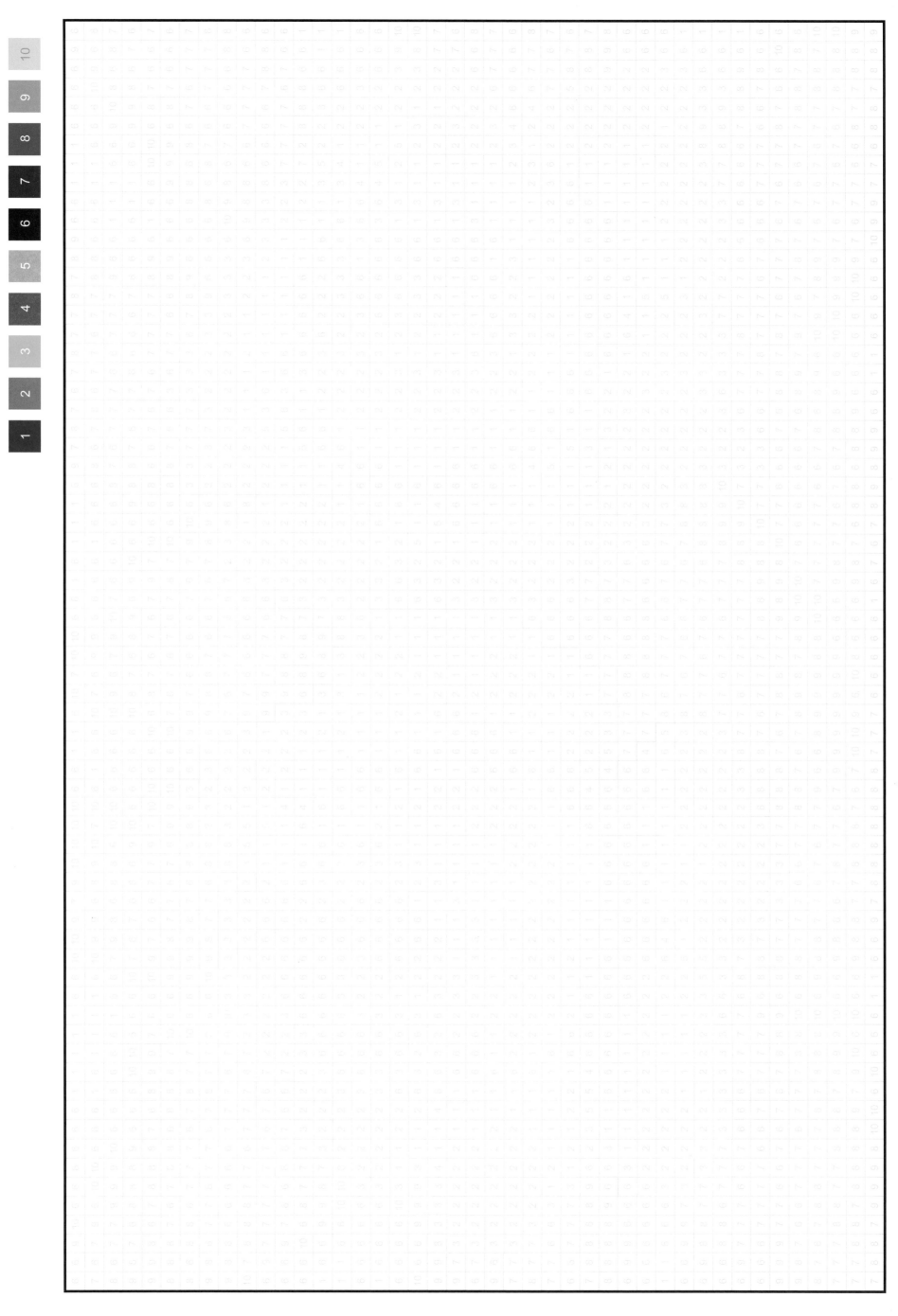

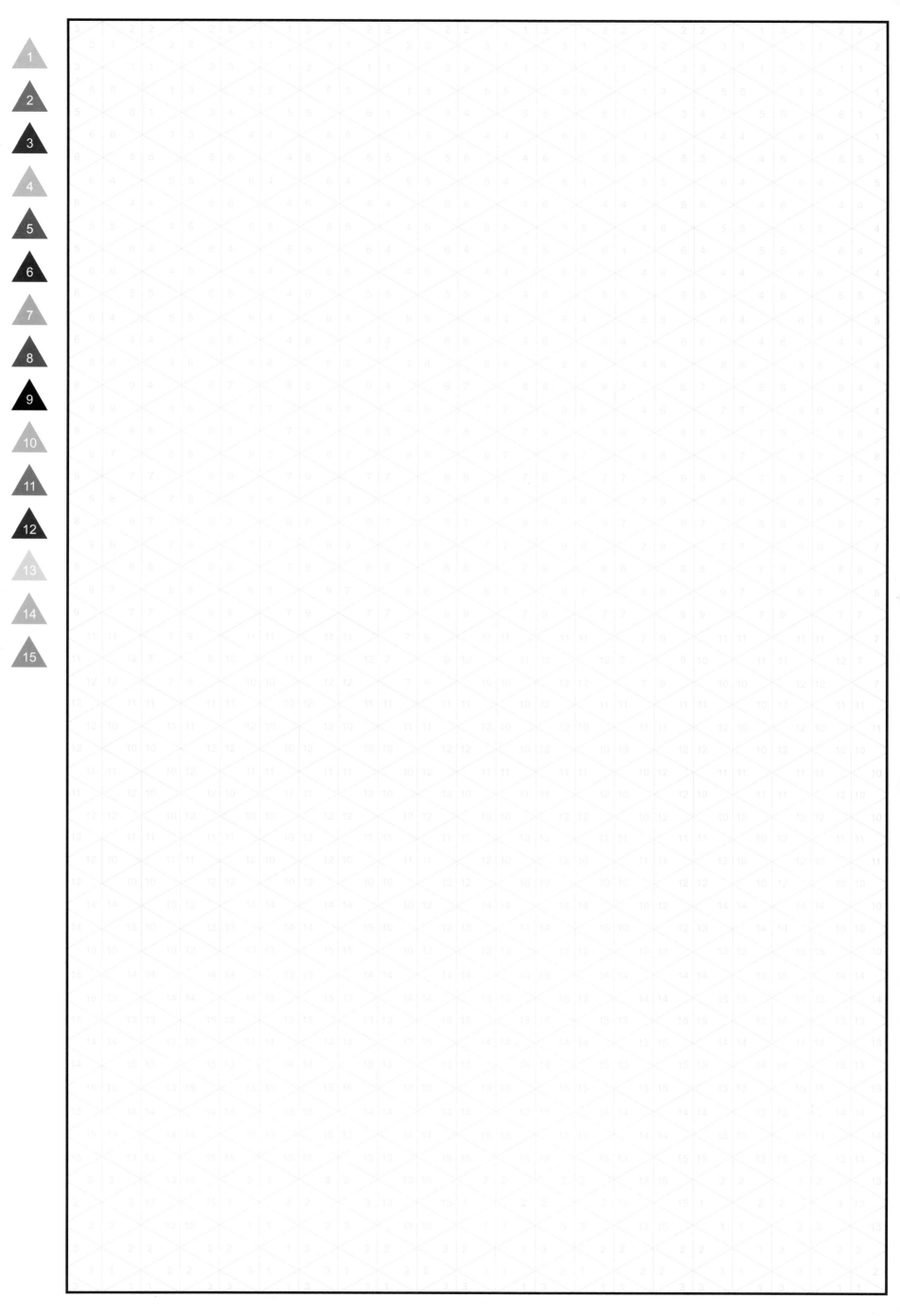

1
2
3
4
5
6
7
8
9
10
11

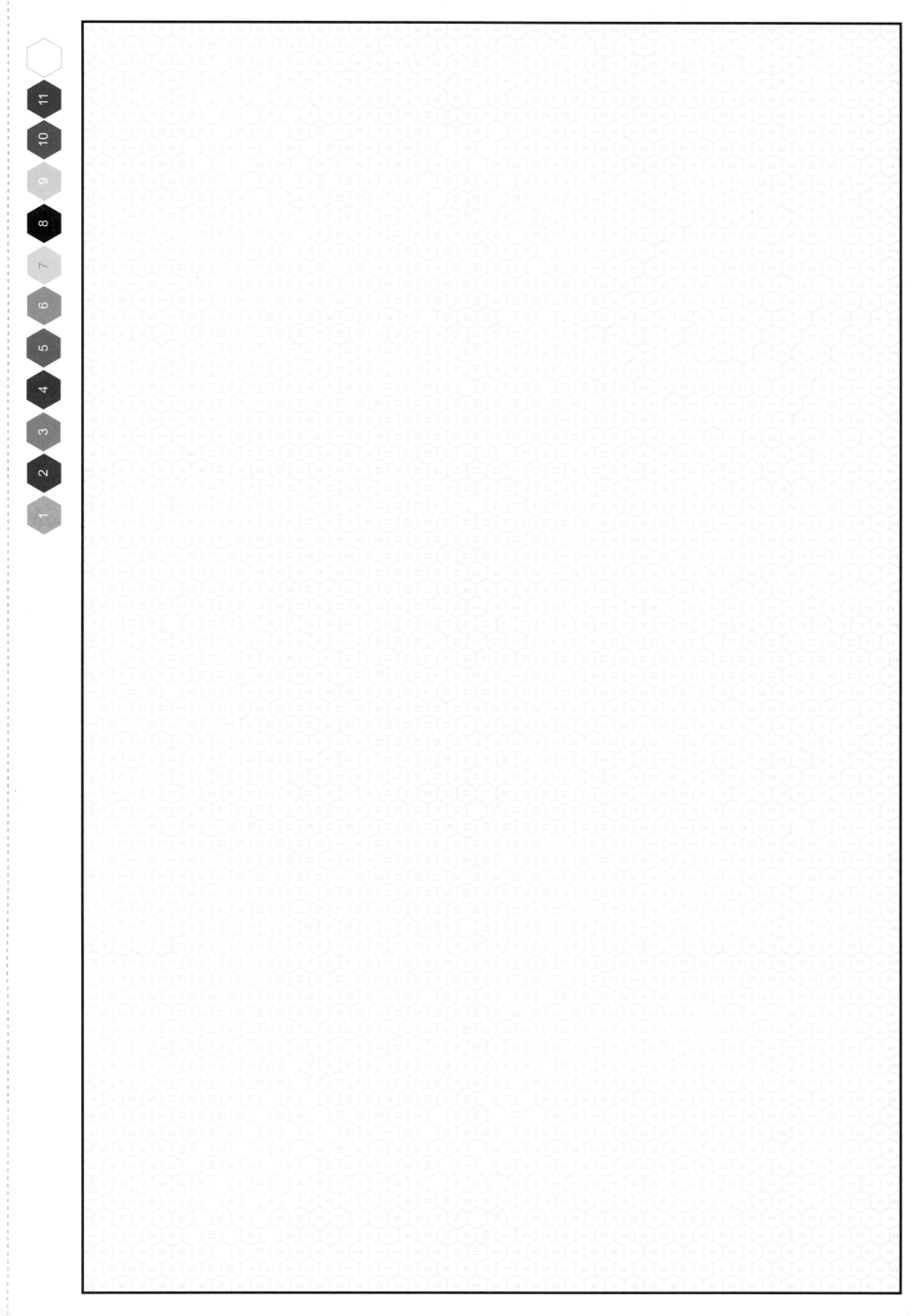

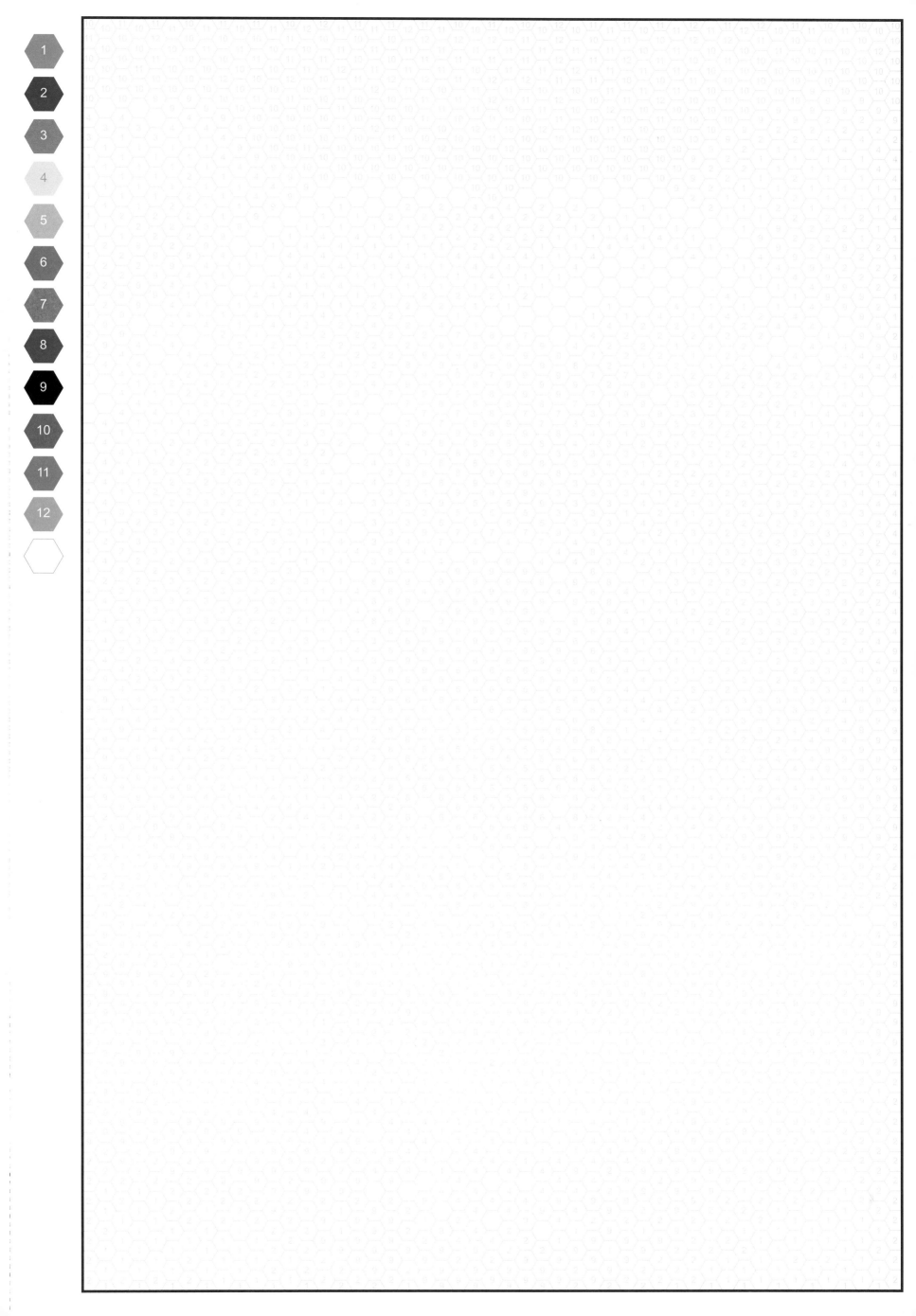

1

2

3

4

5

6

7

8

9

10

11

12

13